Exploring God's Classroom:

A Toddler's Journey

*Your 30-Day
Worldschooling Guide*

Written & Photographed by Sabrina John

Heavenly Home Worldschool

HEAVENLY HOME WORLDSCHOOL

WHERE A SINGLE MOTHER'S NEW FOUND LOVE
FOR
JESUS, TRAVEL, AND BREAD
INSPIRES AN INCREDIBLY UNIQUE
WORLDSCHOOL GUIDE
FOR TODDLERS AS YOUNG AS ONE.

Exploring God's Classroom With Your Toddler

Embark on a beautiful 30-day adventure with your little one, starting as early as one year old! This loving guide is designed to help you both explore and discover a world of wonder and excitement. Together, you'll delve into captivating activities, share heartwarming Biblical stories, and create hands-on experiences that will nurture your toddler's curiosity and fill your hearts with treasured memories. This eBook is your gateway to bonding, learning, and growing together in faith.

Welcome to our Heavenly Home

"What began as a modest 30-day blueprint soon took on a life of its own, blossoming into a 80-page eBook. It was a testament to the divine inspiration that kept my eyes open and my spirit energized during those late-night writing sessions and early morning feeds. This book is more than a guide it's a heartfelt invitation, extended to fellow mothers like myself – women who, despite the whirlwind of responsibilities, share a longing to infuse their children's lives with awe and enlightenment."

Author & Mummy, Sabrina John

COPYRIGHT DISCLAIMER

WELCOME!

We are excited to introduce you to our unique approach to early education, one that not only nurtures the intellectual growth of toddlers but also emphasizes the development of their Godly character within the classroom designed by the Divine.

Join our community of dedicated parents, caregivers, and educators who share the vision of raising children with strong moral values and a profound understanding of the world as God's creation. Our private Facebook group and Instagram page are the perfect places to exchange ideas, experiences, and resources that will enrich your child's spiritual and worldly education.

>> JOIN THE PRIVATE GROUPS

FACEBOOK GROUP
HTTPS://FACEBOOK.COM/GROUPS/118618314672507/
INSTAGRAM PAGE
https://instagram.com/heavenlyhomeworldschool?
igshid=OGQ5ZDc2ODk2ZA==

TABLE OF CONTENTS

HELLO THERE, I'M SABRINA!

For two decades after graduating with a diploma in performing arts in England, I let the wind of adventure guide my path across the United States of America and beyond. From Hollywood, California, to Hackensack, New Jersey, I immersed myself in the world of arts and entertainment. Before becoming a mother, I traveled as a free-spirited artist and writer with my company Sabrina Johns Studios.

But God had a different plan for me. I always dreamed of settling down and homeschooling if I ever met the right man, but my jet-setting lifestyle always kept me running from commitment. When I found myself pregnant, it was a pivotal moment filled with both fear and love. Society tells us we have to choose between our own lifestyle and our baby's life, and I'm so thankful the Holy Spirit was there with me, guiding me from the start. With every beat of my heart, I chose my baby's life and gave up my business and American rock and roll lifestyle to become a mother.

As a single mother, I quickly discovered that I could raise a strong, loving Christian boy with principles and manners. I realized that I could homeschool and satisfy my wanderlust, providing my child with a world-class education through exploration. I embraced homemaking and even became a skilled bread baker. Through Christ, I found the strength not just to survive but to thrive in this new chapter of my life. This is how "HEAVENLY HOME WORLDSCHOOL" began. The dream wasn't over it was just new.

So, while this ebook is not my memoir, my journey is the reason I've created it. I share a glimpse of my story to inspire other mothers. I want you to know that it's possible to homeschool and worldschool even as a single parent. You can be an amazing housewife and provide a nurturing environment for your child, even without a husband, when you have Jesus Christ at the heart of your home. Remember, "I can do all things through Christ who strengthens me." - (Philippians 4:13 NKJV) My journey may not always be a breeze, but it's undeniably a blessing.

Thank you for joining me on this incredible adventure.

Sabrina John

LAUNCHING
INTO LEARNING

"The fear of the LORD is the
beginning of wisdom, And the
knowledge of the Holy One is
understanding." - Proverbs
9:10 (NKJV)

EXPLORING
HOMESCHOOLING METHODS

As a stay-at-home single mum, I'm embarking on a unique educational journey with my child, one that harmoniously blends the beauty of faith, adventure, and knowledge. I'm carving out my own curriculum that best fits my family and lifestyle. I don't believe there is any one right way, and I have let go of the fear that I will do it wrong. Parents are a child's first teacher, after all. But it does help to gather some basic understanding as to what the different terminologies mean. The core of this guide I've created is developing a Christian character but just outside that is our choice of education, a choice that carries profound implications for our little ones lives.

There are a number of different Homeschooling methods see Glossary (pg78) for all definitions. In this chapter, we'll delve into the distinct paths of some of the most known methods, unravelling their unique charms and challenges. As we explore them remember, these methods and approaches can often be combined or adapted based on the unique needs and preferences of the homeschooling or world schooling family. The key is to find an approach that aligns with your educational philosophy and meets the needs of your child.

Let's look into some of the more known of the twenty methods below.

Homeschooling:

Homeschooling is, at its essence, a path of education outside the traditional classroom. For us, it means the freedom to design our curriculum, exploring subjects that align with our values, faith, and interests. As a single parent, homeschooling provides flexibility and the opportunity to cultivate a strong parent-child bond, even in the midst of our world adventures.

Unschooling:

Unschooling is an educational philosophy rooted in the belief that learning should be driven by a child's natural curiosity and interests. This approach allows us to foster a love for learning that is born from the heart. We embrace unschooling as it encourages independence and the pursuit of knowledge based on personal passions.

World Schooling:

World schooling, our most cherished path, marries education with exploration. We journey to far-flung corners of the world, introducing our child to diverse cultures, languages, and histories. The world becomes our classroom, offering lessons that transcend textbooks. Through world schooling, our child develops not only a global perspective but also a deep appreciation for the beauty of God's creation.

Traditional Schooling:

Where a child attends a physical school outside the home, is commonly referred to as "brick-and-mortar schooling" or simply "schooling." It involves students attending a school building with set schedules, classrooms, and a structured curriculum. This is the conventional form of education that most people are familiar with, where students are taught by teachers in a classroom setting.

"FOR THE LORD GIVES WISDOM; FROM HIS MOUTH COME KNOWLEDGE AND UNDERSTANDING."

PROVERBS 2:6 (NKJV)

"As a single mother, the decision to choose homeschooling for my child has been deeply rooted in faith and love. I firmly believe that with God's guidance, I can provide not only a strong academic foundation but also instill essential Christian values and principles in my child's life. Homeschooling allows us to create a nurturing and spiritually rich environment, where we can pray together, study the Bible, and explore the wonders of God's creation. While it may seem like a daunting task to do it all, I draw strength from my faith and the unwavering support of my Heavenly Father. With His grace, I can embrace this journey of single parenthood and homeschooling, knowing that I am shaping my child's future with love, faith, and a whole lot of trust in His divine plan."

- Sabrina John

MONTESSORI AND MASON METHODS

At Heavenly Home Worldschool, we marry unschool, home and world and use the terminology homeschooling or worldschooling interchangeably. We draw inspiration from the Maria Montessori and Charlotte Mason philosophies. These educational approaches resonate with me as a full time parent, and they align perfectly with our worldschooling adventures. The Montessori method's emphasis on hands-on, self-directed learning mirrors the way I guide my child through our explorations. Charlotte Mason's principles of living books, nature studies, and narration complement my journey as a parent, nurturing not only my child's intellect but also their character and faith.

I find a lot of wisdom in the writings of Ellen G. White also, and her insights about homemaking and schooling resonate deeply with our educational philosophy at Heavenly Home Worldschool.

These three voices - Maria Montessori, Charlotte Mason, and Ellen G. White - guide both my personal path as a parent and our mission at Heavenly Home Worldschool I give myself the freedom to adapt them to best fit my individual family.

We are proud of this unique educational approach, one that blends these philosophies to nurture not only children's minds but also their hearts and spirits. In our company, we aim to create an educational journey that is both enriching and faith-filled. We enjoy alternating between these approaches when planning activities, ensuring a well-rounded and holistic learning experience for the families we serve.

> EDUCATION IS AN ATMOSPHERE, A DISCIPLINE, A LIFE. THE MOTHER IS NOT A PERSON TO LEAN ON, BUT A PERSON TO MAKE LEANING UNNECESSARY."
>
> - CHARLOTTE MASON

GOD'S MAGNIFICENT CLASSROOM

Undoubtedly, the world crafted by the hand of God is the most magnificent classroom of all. Immersed in the embrace of nature, a child has the opportunity to explore the realms of geography, biology, botany, geology, and countless other subjects. The marvels of creation reveal themselves in captivating ways, guiding us through the fundamental subjects of Montessori homeschooling.

CHARACTER COMES FIRST

Instilling strong character traits in your toddler is the key to fostering trust and love, ultimately connecting them with God's boundless love.

The Foundation of Character

At the heart of our homeschooling journey is the belief that a child's character is their most valuable asset. We may not claim to be Montessori homeschooling masters, but we do believe that character development starts from the very beginning. Just as we nourish their bodies with healthy food, we must also nurture their hearts and minds.

Character is about more than just good behavior. It encompasses qualities like kindness, empathy, honesty, and patience. These virtues lay the foundation for a strong moral compass that will guide your child throughout their life.

Teaching Through Example

One of the most powerful ways to teach character is by example. Your child watches your every move, and they learn from how you interact with them, others, and the world around you. Show them what it means to be compassionate, forgiving, and loving in your daily actions.

Trust and Love

Trust and love are the cornerstones of our teaching journey. When your child trusts you, they are more receptive to the lessons you impart. Creating a loving and secure environment fosters this trust. Spend quality time with your child, engage in play, sing, read stories, and let them know they are cherished.

The Role of Faith

As Christian homeschoolers, faith plays a central role in our lives. We seek to pass down the teachings of our faith to our children, nurturing their spiritual growth. Incorporating prayer, Bible stories, songs, and discussions about God's love into your daily routine can instill a deep sense of faith in your child.

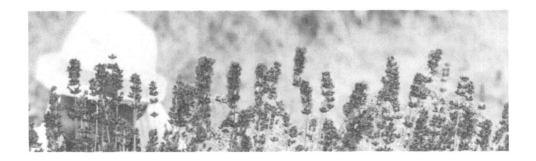

The Daily Planner

Our daily planner isn't just a schedule; it's a source of motivation and inspiration. It helps us structure our days with purpose, ensuring there's time for learning, faith-building activities, and, certainly lots of, fun. You'll find that having a plan in place makes homeschooling more manageable and enjoyable for both you and your child.

Sharing Our Guide

This guide is a labor of love, created from Sabrina's own experiences and the desire to share what she has learned with fellow homeschooling parents. We may not have a multitude of university PHDs, or all the answers, but we're here to support and encourage you on this incredible journey of faith-based homeschooling. Together, we can raise children who are not only academically equipped but most importantly spiritually grounded, confident, and filled with love.

In the chapters that follow, we'll dive deeper into practical tips and activities to help you instill character, faith, and love in your child. Remember, you are your child's first and most influential teacher, and with faith as your guide, you can lead them toward a brighter future filled with God's love.

Guided by Scripture

As we navigate our homeschooling journey, we are reminded
of the wisdom found in Ellen White's 'Child Guidance,' in
which expands on Proverbs 22:6: 'Train up a child in the way
he should go; and when he is old, he will not depart from it.'
This timeless message emphasizes our role as parents goes
beyond mere words; it's about showing and demonstrating to
our children the way to go through our actions. Remember, it
says 'train,' signifying the importance of demonstrating
rather than just telling our children the way they should go,
and there's a profound reason for that.

FUN FACT

Did you know that a child's
brain forms most of its neural
connections by the age of
three? This early period of
brain development is when
character traits like empathy,
kindness, and resilience can
have a profound and lasting
impact on their personality.

HEAVENLY HOME
WORLDSCHOOL BEGINS

Heavenly Home World School took flight through the passionate vision of Sabrina John, a devoted mother. This initiative offers invaluable guidance to stay-at-home mums, illuminating a faith-based world schooling approach designed for children as young as one year old. Drawing inspiration from her personal journey as a single mother and unwavering commitment to create a nurturing environment firmly rooted in God's teachings, she fondly refers to it as 'God's classroom.'

Within this educational journey, Sabrina seamlessly weaves Montessori principles into the fabric of monthly activities, fostering a harmonious blend of Christian character building, Montessori methodology, and Charlotte Mason's educational philosophy. This unique fusion empowers young learners with a comprehensive and faith-centered educational experience.

Sabrina, reflects on her vision: "I just knew in my heart that I wanted to give my son a unique education, one woven from the threads of our travels and life's experiences. My love for exploring new places and cultures was like a compass guiding me towards worldschooling. Why wait, I thought, why not start this incredible journey when he's just a year old, learning from God's magnificent world?"

EVERY DAY IS
AN OPPORTUNITY
TO NURTURE
YOUR CHILD'S
FAITH AND
CURIOSITY IN THE
WORLD AROUND
THEM.

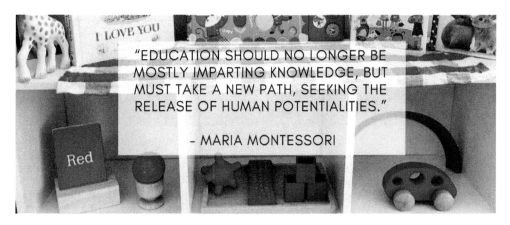

"EDUCATION SHOULD NO LONGER BE MOSTLY IMPARTING KNOWLEDGE, BUT MUST TAKE A NEW PATH, SEEKING THE RELEASE OF HUMAN POTENTIALITIES."

- MARIA MONTESSORI

THE 8 MONTESSORI CORE SUBJECTS

children engage in activities that nurture vital life skills, such as pouring, dressing, cleaning, and food preparation. These practical tasks foster independence, enhance fine motor skills, and promote focused concentration.

2. Sensory Exploration: Montessori's sensory materials are thoughtfully designed to refine a child's senses and provide a foundation for comprehending abstract concepts like size, shape, texture, and colour. This sensory foundation serves as a stepping stone for later mathematical and geometric understanding.

3. Language Development: Language holds a prominent place in Montessori education. Children embark on their reading and writing journey using phonetic tools and hands-on materials such as sandpaper letters and the movable alphabet. The curriculum also encourages storytelling and meaningful conversations.

4. Mathematical Discovery: The Montessori math materials are concrete and tactile, enabling children to explore mathematical concepts through hands-on activities. Their progression spans from a concrete understanding (through

manipulation) to an abstract grasp (using symbols) of numbers and mathematical operations.

5. Cultural Exploration: Cultural studies encompass subjects like geography, history, botany, zoology, and the physical sciences. Children are invited to discover the world around them through hands-on materials, maps, and globes, fostering a sense of connection to the broader world.

6. Scientific Inquiry: Montessori classrooms often emphasize science education, encouraging children to explore and experiment with natural phenomena. This may involve the study of plants, animals, weather patterns, and various scientific principles.

7. Creative Expression through Art and Music: While not considered traditional core subjects, Montessori education places significant value on creative expression. Children are encouraged to explore art and music through diverse activities, nurturing their innate creativity and self-expression.

8. Peaceful Hearts and Minds: A distinctive aspect of Montessori education is its emphasis on peace education. This encompasses social and emotional development, conflict resolution, and the cultivation of empathy and peaceful interactions among children. It often includes discussions on respecting others and fostering a harmonious relationship with the environment.

TAILORING PRINCIPLES FOR YOUR TODDLER

In our enriching homeschooling journey, these principles gently guide us, more as compass directions than rigid boundaries. They offer valuable wisdom, yet we hold dear the importance of adaptability. Each child, a unique and cherished creation, possesses their own interests, strengths, and pace of learning. Thus, we whole-heartedly embrace the flexibility to craft lessons and activities that align with our child's individual journey, recognizing their path of discovery as unique as the fingerprints upon their hearts.

Before we dive into this journey, I wish to leave you with an essential reminder. It might appear as though there's an abundance to tackle, but there's truly no rush. Take your time, adapting the tasks not just for your child but for yourself as well. Managing a household is a full-time role in itself, and there's no need to press yourself beyond measure. Revel in these precious moments and avoid getting too entangled in over-planning every minute.

As we commence this voyage, let's draw inspiration from the timeless wisdom found in Scripture: 'I can do all things through Christ who strengthens me.' (Philippians 4:13) With this steadfast guiding principle, before we begin our 30 day plan let's have a look in to toys. After all a child's work is play especially at this tender age of life.

LET'S TALK ABOUT TOYS

Maria Montessori had specific views on toys and their role in a child's development. She believed that toys should be carefully chosen and designed to support a child's learning and development. Montessori's approach to toys is rooted in the idea that toys should be educational, purposeful, and aligned with a child's developmental stage. Here are a few key points she made about toys:

Purposeful Toys:

Montessori advocated for toys that have a clear purpose and encourage meaningful engagement. She believed that toys should serve a specific educational function, helping children develop important skills and concepts..

Simple and Natural:

Montessori preferred toys that are simple, made from natural materials, and free from excessive decoration or noise. This allows children to focus on the sensory aspects of the materials and encourages a connection to the natural world.

Open-Ended Materials:

Montessori encouraged the use of open-ended materials that can be used in a variety of ways, allowing children to use their creativity and imagination. These materials promote exploration and problem-solving.

REAL-LIFE REPLICAS:

Montessori often used real-life replicas or "miniatures" as toys, such as animals, vehicles, and child-sized brooms, utensils, or tools. These toys help children engage in practical life activities and develop fine motor skills.

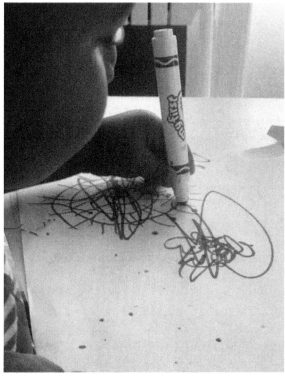

DEVELOPMENTAL APPROPRIATENESS:

Montessori stressed the importance of choosing toys that are appropriate for a child's developmental stage. Toys should challenge children but not frustrate them.

TOY
SUGGESTIONS

Purposeful Toys:

1. Puzzle Sets: Wooden or cardboard puzzles that require problem-solving and matching skills can be excellent for promoting cognitive development.

2. Building Blocks: Classic wooden building blocks allow children to explore engineering and spatial concepts while fostering creativity.

3. Math Manipulatives: Toys like counting beads or number cards can help children learn mathematical concepts through hands-on exploration.

Simple and Natural:

1. Wooden Stacking Rings: These simple, wooden toys promote hand-eye coordination and fine motor skills without distractions.

2. Natural Fiber Dolls: Dolls made from cloth and stuffed with natural fibers provide a tactile experience and encourage imaginative play.

3. Woven Baskets: Children can use these baskets for organizing toys or exploring textures, and they fit well with a natural aesthetic.

Open-Ended Materials:

1. Play Silks: These colorful, silky fabrics can become anything a child imagines, from capes to rivers in a pretend play scenario.

2. Modeling Clay: Non-toxic, open-ended play lets children sculpt and create a wide range of shapes and objects.

3. Loose Parts: Collect items like seashells, stones, or wooden beads to encourage open-ended creativity and sensory exploration.

Real-Life Replicas:

1. Child-Sized Kitchen Utensils: Miniature cooking tools, pots, and pans can help children learn practical life skills and engage in cooking pretend play.
2. Gardening Tools: Child-sized shovels, rakes, and watering cans can promote an understanding of gardening and outdoor activities.
3. Cleaning Set: Miniature brooms, mops, and dustpans encourage children to participate in household chores and develop fine motor skills.

Developmental Appropriateness:

1. Baby Rattles: For infants, soft rattles with contrasting colors and textures provide sensory stimulation.
2. Shape Sorters: Toddlers can benefit from shape-sorting toys that challenge their cognitive and motor skills without overwhelming them.
3. Art Supplies: Older children might enjoy age-appropriate art materials like colored pencils, safety scissors, and washable paints for creative expression.

These are just suggestions. The key thing to remember when it comes to toys is to choose those that align with a child's age and developmental stage while encouraging learning and play.

KEEP IT SIMPLE
...You Are ENOUGH!

♻Caring for God's Earth♻

Crafting your own toys from recycled or upcycled materials found in your home is not only a creative and cost-effective endeavor but also instills in children a sense of stewardship for God's planet, emphasizing the value of creative reuse and sustainability. By reimagining everyday items into toys, we not only encourage their creativity but also impart the value of resourcefulness and eco-consciousness, honoring the world that God has blessed us with.

In the realm of Christian worldschooling, there's no need for parents to feel compelled to invest in opulent wooden toys and Instagram-worthy shelving. The true essence of learning lies not in the aesthetic appeal of possessions but in the nurturing of a rich and immersive environment. Embrace the joy of crafting your own toys together with your child, using everyday items at hand. Often, the most treasured educational experiences emerge from these creative endeavors. It's a reminder that the young, inquisitive hearts of our children find wonder in the simple things, the real items they discover within the comforting walls of their home. In this journey, the focus is not on lavish displays but on cultivating a space where curiosity and exploration are celebrated, where faith, love, and learning are intertwined in beautiful, authentic ways.

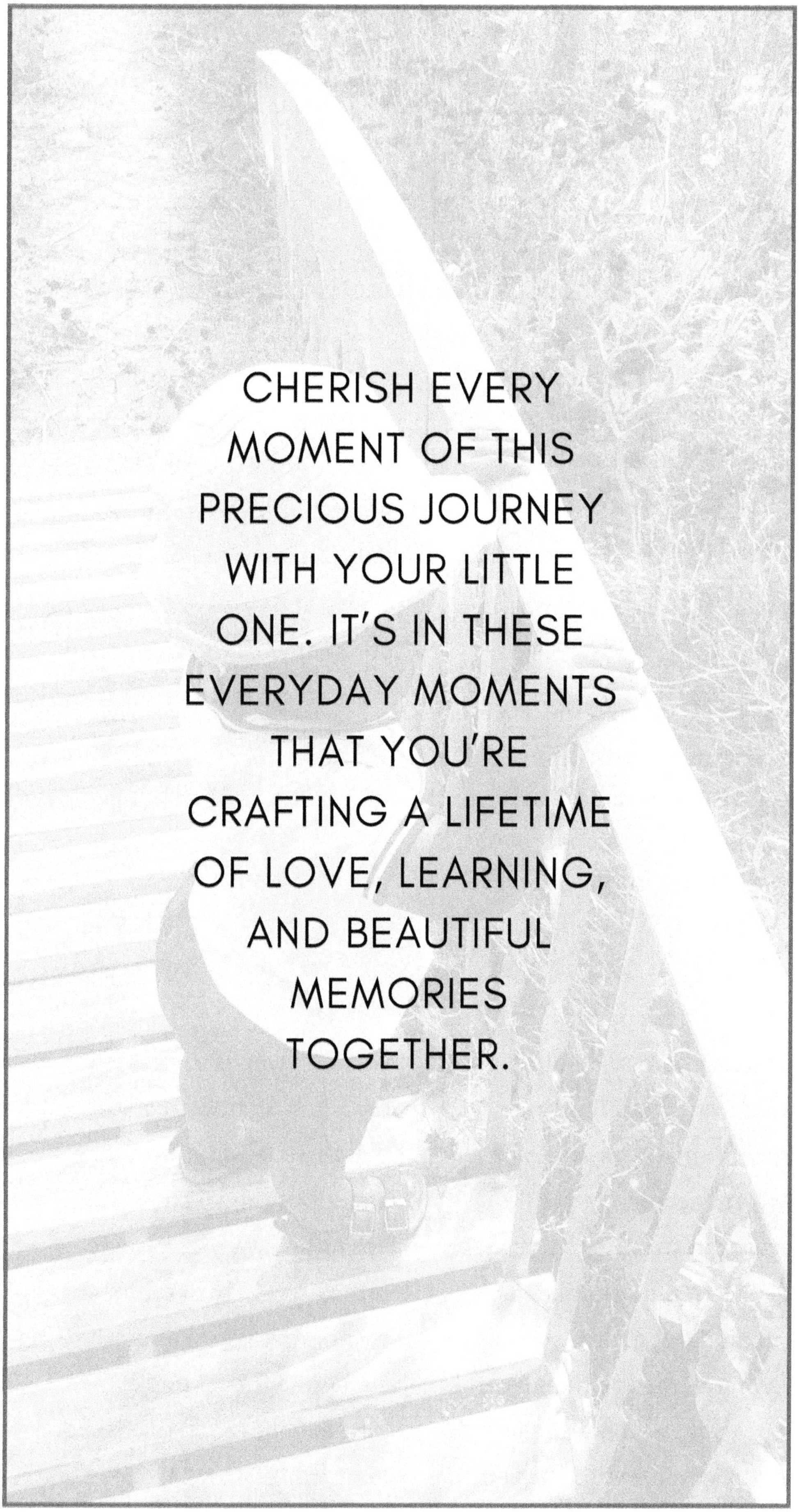

CHERISH EVERY
MOMENT OF THIS
PRECIOUS JOURNEY
WITH YOUR LITTLE
ONE. IT'S IN THESE
EVERYDAY MOMENTS
THAT YOU'RE
CRAFTING A LIFETIME
OF LOVE, LEARNING,
AND BEAUTIFUL
MEMORIES
TOGETHER.

HAPPY DAY

Celebrating Sabbath

"I'm discovering how to cherish and truly value this incredible day of God-given rest. It provides me with a beautiful reason to just pause. During my turbulent pregnancy through to postpartum, it gave me renewed life and strength to face another week head-on as a single mother. To this day, I honestly believe I can achieve so much, all thanks to the profound impact of this special day." - Sabrina John

As you embark on your Sabbath journey, I encourage you to explore Week 1: Introduction to Nature - Sabbath Rest Suggestions. These activities will help you connect with the wonders of the natural world and deepen your appreciation for this special day.

* * * *

The Sabbath day is indeed a sacred and beautiful time to rest, reflect, and express gratitude for the blessings we've received. It's a time-honored tradition to gather with loved ones and share meaningful meals, such as my homemade Challahs and Focaccia, which bring joy and excitement to the table.

For full recipes and video tutorials on how to create delightful Sabbath breads, and all of the 30 days activities, we recommend following @sabrinajohn.co on her Instagram and other social media channels @HeavenlyHomeWorldschool

The
30 Day
Plan

INTRODUCTION TO NATURE
WEEK 1

DAY 1: NATURE WALK

Activity: Begin your worldschooling journey with a gentle nature walk. Explore your surroundings, noticing the beauty of God's creations. Talk to your toddler about the colors, shapes, and sounds you encounter. Encourage curiosity and wonder.

What You Need:

• Comfortable walking shoes for both you and your toddler.
• A small bag or basket for collecting natural treasures like leaves or rocks. (keep in mind that leaves may decay quickly and crumble before tomorrow's journal session)

Benefits/Skills Developed:

1. Observation Skills: Your toddler will learn to observe and appreciate the world around them, fostering a keen sense of curiosity.
2. Language Development: Through conversation during the walk, your child's vocabulary and language skills will improve as they describe what they see.

"YOU'RE NURTURING A LITTLE EXPLORER WHO'S DISCOVERING GOD'S WONDERS."

INTRODUCTION TO NATURE
WEEK 1

DAY 2: NATURE JOURNAL

Activity: Start a nature journal together. Use crayons or colored pencils to draw or paste leaves and flowers collected from the previous day's walk. This activity encourages creativity and fine motor skills.

What You Need:

- Drawing materials like crayons or colored pencils.
- Glue and child-safe scissors.
- Your nature treasures from Day 1.

Benefits/Skills Developed:

1. Creativity: Keeping a nature journal helps nurture your toddler's creative expression as they engage with the natural world through art.
2. Fine Motor Skills: Activities like coloring and cutting improve their hand-eye coordination and fine motor skills.

"EVERY NATURE WALK IS A STEP CLOSER TO UNDERSTANDING GOD'S CREATION."

INTRODUCTION TO NATURE
WEEK 1

DAY 3: BIBLE STORY TIME

Activity: Dive into the Bible with your toddler by reading about God's creation of the world in Genesis 1. Discuss the importance of taking care of the Earth as stewards of God's gifts.

What You Need:

• A child-friendly Bible or Bible storybook.
• A comfortable reading spot for you and your toddler.

Benefits/Skills Developed:

1. Spiritual Awareness: Introducing your toddler to biblical stories helps them develop a sense of spirituality and understanding of faith.
2. Comprehension and Listening Skills: Listening to stories and discussing their meaning enhances your child's comprehension and listening skills.

"NATURE IS GOD'S CLASSROOM, AND YOU'RE THE BEST TEACHER THEY COULD HAVE."

INTRODUCTION TO NATURE
WEEK 1

DAY 4: PLANTING A SEED

Activity: Teach your toddler about growth and responsibility by planting a seed in a small pot. Demonstrate how to water and care for it, emphasizing the importance of nurturing life.

What You Need:

• A small pot or container.
• Soil and a seed suitable for easy growth, like a sunflower or bean seed.
• A watering can or spray bottle.

Benefits/Skills Developed:

1. Responsibility: Caring for the plant fosters a sense of responsibility as your toddler takes on the role of a caregiver.
2. Understanding of Growth: This activity introduces the concept of growth and life cycles, helping your child comprehend the natural world.

"YOU'RE PLANTING SEEDS OF KNOWLEDGE AND FAITH IN YOUR TODDLER'S HEART."

INTRODUCTION TO NATURE
WEEK 1

DAY 5: PICNIC & PARK

Activity: Celebrate your week of nature exploration with a fun outdoor picnic and playtime in the park. Let your toddler run, explore, and enjoy the beauty of the outdoors.

What You Need:

• Picnic essentials like a blanket, snacks, and drinks.
• Outdoor toys or balls for playtime.

Benefits/Skills Developed:

1. Physical Development: Outdoor play promotes physical development, including motor skills and physical fitness.
2. Social Skills: Interaction with other children at the park encourages social development and sharing.

"YOUR JOURNEY IN WORLDSCHOOLING IS A BEAUTIFUL BLEND OF FAITH AND EXPLORATION."

DAY 6/7: RESET & REST

Introduction to Nature - Sabbath Suggestions

1. **Nature Sabbath Walk:** Take a peaceful Sabbath walk in a local park or garden. Reflect on the beauty of God's creation.

2. **Nature-Inspired Crafts:** Spend the afternoon creating nature-inspired crafts together, like pressed flower art or leaf collages.

3. **Bible Story Time:** Share a special Bible story related to creation and discuss its significance during your Sabbath meal.

4. **Challah Flavor:** Enjoy a honey and oat challah to symbolize the sweetness and nourishment of God's creation.

5. **Focaccia Flavor.** Fig and Honey.

Full Recipe and video tutorials on our social media handles.

"SABBATH REMINDS ME THAT I AM NOT ALONE IN MY JOURNEY AS A MOTHER; GOD IS WITH ME EVERY STEP OF THE WAY."

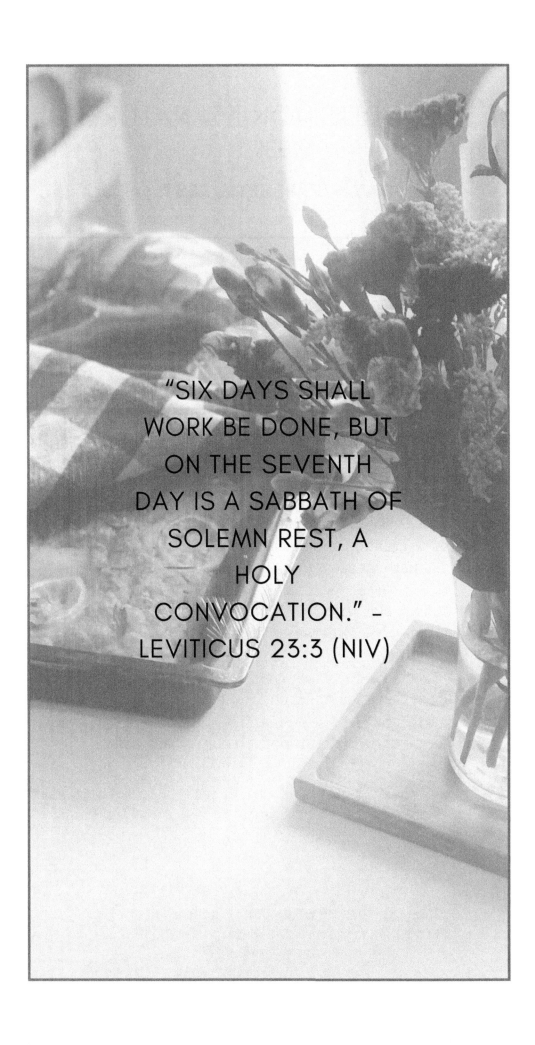

"SIX DAYS SHALL WORK BE DONE, BUT ON THE SEVENTH DAY IS A SABBATH OF SOLEMN REST, A HOLY CONVOCATION." - LEVITICUS 23:3 (NIV)

LEARNING ABOUT ANIMALS
WEEK 2

DAY 8: VISIT A PETTING ZOO OR FARM

Activity: Take your toddler to a petting zoo or farm to observe and interact with animals. Discuss the various animals and their characteristics.

What You Need:

• Admission tickets or farm entrance fees.
• Comfortable clothing suitable for outdoor activities.

Benefits/Skills Developed:

1. Animal Knowledge: Your child will learn about different animals and their behaviors.
2. Empathy: Interacting with animals fosters empathy and care for living creatures.

"TEACHING YOUR CHILD ABOUT GOD'S ANIMALS IS A GIFT THAT IGNITES A LIFELONG CONNECTION TO HIS LIVING WONDERS."

LEARNING ABOUT ANIMALS
WEEK 2

DAY 9: ANIMAL SOUND CHARADES

Activity: Play a fun game of animal charades as a family. Take turns acting out animal sounds and guessing the animals.

What You Need:

• A list of animal names for charades.
• Creativity and enthusiasm!

Benefits/Skills Developed:

1. Communication Skills: Sound Charades enhance verbal communication and creativity.
2. Teamwork: Playing as a family encourages cooperation and teamwork.

"CREATIVITY BLOSSOMS WHEN WE MARVEL AT THE ARTISTRY OF GOD'S ANIMAL WORLD."

LEARNING ABOUT ANIMALS
WEEK 2

DAY 10: BIBLE STORY - NOAH'S ARK

Activity: Read the story of Noah's Ark from the Bible and discuss the importance of taking care of animals and God's creation.

What You Need:

• A child-friendly Bible or Bible storybook.
• A comfortable reading spot for you and your toddler.

Benefits/Skills Developed:

1. Values and Morals: Understanding the story of Noah's Ark teaches values of compassion and care for animals.
2. Spiritual Growth: Discussing biblical stories deepens spiritual awareness.

"YOU'RE NOT JUST TEACHING; YOU'RE BUILDING A FIRM FOUNDATION OF FAITH AND KNOWLEDGE, USING GOD'S ANIMALS AS YOUR TOOLS."

LEARNING ABOUT ANIMALS
WEEK 2

DAY 11: ANIMAL CRAFTS

Activity: Create animal-themed crafts together, such as paper plate masks or finger-paint animal prints.

What You Need:

• Craft supplies like paper plates, paint, markers, and glue.
• Creativity and imagination.

Benefits/Skills Developed:

1. Creativity: Crafting fosters creative expression and fine motor skills.
2. Imagination: Imagining and making animal-themed crafts promotes imaginative thinking.

"EACH CREATURE IS A CHAPTER IN THE BEAUTIFUL STORY OF GOD'S CREATION, AND YOU'RE THE STORYTELLER SHARING IT WITH YOUR CHILD."

LEARNING ABOUT ANIMALS
WEEK 2

DAY 12: ANIMAL SCAVENGER HUNT

Activity: Go on an animal scavenger hunt in your backyard or a nearby nature reserve. Look for signs of animals, like footprints or nests.

What You Need:

• A list of animals to search for.
• Binoculars, magnifying glass, or a notebook for observations.

Benefits/Skills Developed:

1. Observation Skills: Scavenger hunts improve observation and attention to detail.
2. Outdoor Exploration: Encourages outdoor exploration and connection with nature.

We have a Free Downloadable Print out Animal Scavenger Hunt game on our website if needed.

"THROUGH ANIMALS, WE GLIMPSE THE COMPASSION OF JESUS, WHO CHERISHED ALL CREATION."

LEARNING ABOUT ANIMALS
WEEK 2

DAY 13/14 RESET & REST

Learning About Animals - Sabbath Suggestions

1. **Visit an Animal Sanctuary:** Visit an animal sanctuary or rescue center and discuss the importance of caring for God's creatures.

2. **Animal Charades:** Play a fun game of animal charades as a family after your Sabbath meal.

3. **Bible Story Time:** Read about Noah's Ark and the covenant with animals in Genesis 9. Reflect on our responsibility to care for them.

4. **Challah Flavor:** Bake a challah with seeds (e.g., sesame or poppy seeds) to symbolize the variety of creatures on Earth.

5. **Focaccia Flavor:** Bake a sun-dried tomato and basil focaccia with a sprinkle of mixed seeds to symbolize the diversity of creatures on Earth.

"IN THE SACRED RHYTHM OF THE SABBATH, SINGLE MOTHERS FIND SOLACE, A MOMENT TO BREATHE, AND THE RESILIENCE TO RISE ABOVE LIFE'S STORMS."

"COME TO ME, ALL YOU WHO ARE WEARY AND BURDENED, AND I WILL GIVE YOU REST."

- MATTHEW 11:28

EXPLORING THE SEASONS
WEEK 3

DAY 15: SEASONAL WEATHER REFLECTION

Activity: Spend the day reflecting on the current season and its unique features. Talk about the weather and changes in nature.

What You Need:

• A cozy spot for discussions.
• Seasonal decorations or artwork to set the mood.

Benefits/Skills Developed:

1. Seasonal Awareness: Helps your child understand and appreciate the changing seasons.
2. Communication Skills: Encourages discussions and sharing of thoughts.

"WITH EACH SEASON'S EMBRACE, NATURE PAINTS A NEW CHAPTER, REMINDING US OF LIFE'S BEAUTIFUL TRANSFORMATIONS."

EXPLORING THE SEASONS
WEEK 3

DAY 16: SEASONAL FAMILY PHOTO

Activity: Take a family photo outdoors to capture the beauty of the current season. Discuss what you see in the photo.

What You Need:

• A camera or smartphone for photos.
• Seasonal clothing or props for the photo.

Benefits/Skills Developed:

1. Memory-Making: Creating seasonal family photos is a wonderful way to build lasting memories.
2. Observation and Conversation: Discussing the photo encourages observation and conversation.

"AS THE SEASONS CHANGE, SO DOES THE CANVAS OF OUR WORLD, REVEALING GOD'S ARTISTRY IN EVERY SHIFT."

EXPLORING THE SEASONS
WEEK 3

DAY 17: BIBLE STORY - ECCLESIASTES 3:1-8

Activity: Read Ecclesiastes 3:1-8, which talks about seasons in life, and discuss its meaning in the context of changing seasons.

What You Need:

• A Bible or Bible verse printout.
• A comfortable reading and discussion space.

Benefits/Skills Developed:

1. Spiritual Growth: Exploring biblical wisdom deepens spiritual awareness and understanding.
2. Life Lessons: Discussing the passage introduces valuable life lessons about change and acceptance.

"JUST AS THE SEASONS SHIFT, SO DO THE SEASONS OF OUR LIVES, EACH BRINGING ITS OWN BLESSINGS AND LESSONS."

EXPLORING THE SEASONS
WEEK 3

DAY 18: SEASONAL FOOD OBSERVATIONS

Activity: Explore seasonal fruits or vegetables by planting them if you have a garden, or by visiting a grocery store to observe and select them.

What You Need:

For Garden Option:
• Seasonal fruit or vegetable seeds.
• Gardening tools (small shovel, watering can, pots).
• Soil or gardening space.

For Grocery Store Option:
• A list of seasonal fruits or vegetables to observe and select.
• A trip to a local grocery store.

Benefits/Skills Developed:

1. Gardening Skills (for those with a garden): Provides an introduction to basic gardening skills and an appreciation for growing seasonal produce.
2. Responsibility (for those with a garden): Caring for plants teaches responsibility and nurturing.

3. Seasonal Food Awareness (for grocery store option): Helps families become more aware of seasonal fruits and vegetables available at the grocery store, promoting healthy eating habits and food awareness.

"GOD'S SEASONAL BOUNTY, A FLAVORFUL REMINDER OF HIS PROVIDENCE, ENRICHES OUR LIVES WITH NATURE'S BLESSINGS."

EXPLORING THE SEASONS
WEEK 3

DAY 19: SEASONAL NATURE WALK

Activity: Go for a nature walk and observe how the environment changes with the seasons. Look for seasonal plants and animals.

What You Need:

• Season-appropriate clothing for outdoor walks.
• Binoculars or magnifying glass for closer observations.

Benefits/Skills Developed:

1. Environmental Awareness: Promotes an understanding of the impact of seasons on nature.
2. Outdoor Exploration: Encourages outdoor exploration and connection with the environment.

"WALKING IS A SACRED ACT, A CHANCE TO CONNECT WITH THE WORLD AND WITH GOD, STEP BY STEP, MOMENT BY MOMENT."

EXPLORING THE SEASONS
WEEK 3

DAY 20/21: RESET & REST

Exploring the Seasons - Sabbath Rest Suggestions

1. **Seasonal Reflection:** Spend the Sabbath reflecting on the changing seasons and how they mirror life's rhythms.

2. **Seasonal Family Photo:** Take a family photo outdoors to capture the beauty of the current season.

3. **Bible Story Time:** Read Ecclesiastes 3:1-8 and discuss the significance of life's different seasons.

4. **Challah Flavor:** Bake a cinnamon and apple challah to celebrate the flavors of the current season.

5. **Focaccia Flavor.** Create a caramelized pear and cinnamon focaccia to celebrate the rich and warm flavors of the current season.

"AFTER TOILING TIRELESSLY THROUGHOUT THE WEEK, STAY-AT-HOME MOTHERS CHERISH THE SABBATH'S RESPITE, A DAY WHEN THEIR UNWAVERING DEDICATION FINDS ITS WELL-DESERVED REST."

"SABBATH IS A TIME TO
CELEBRATE WHAT IS TRULY
IMPORTANT IN LIFE – THE
PEOPLE WE LOVE, THE
BEAUTY THAT SURROUNDS
US, AND THE CREATOR
WHO MADE IT ALL."

ART AND CREATIVITY
WEEK 4

DAY 22: ART STATION SET UP

Activity: Start the week by setting up a family art station together. Explore a variety of supplies to spark creativity.

What You Need:

- A wide range of art supplies.
- An open and imaginative mindset.

Benefits/Skills Developed:

1. Creativity: Crafting allows for creative expression and exploration.
2. Fine Motor Skills: Art and craft activities enhance fine motor skills and coordination.

"TODDLERS EXPRESS GOD'S WORLD THROUGH ART."

ARTS AND CREATIVITY
WEEK 4

DAY 23: PAINT A RAINBOW

Activity: Create a beautiful rainbow together, exploring the magic of mixing and blending colors.

What You Need:

- Watercolor paints, brushes.
- Large sheets of paper.
- Enthusiasm for vibrant colors.

Benefits/Skills Developed:

1. Color Exploration: Learn about colors and their combinations.
2. Fine Motor Skills: Painting improves hand-eye coordination.

"ART IS OUR WAY OF JOINING GOD IN THE ACT OF CREATION, PAINTING OUR STORIES ON THE CANVAS OF HIS WORLD."

ARTS AND CREATIVITY
WEEK 4

DAY 24: BIBLE STORY - PSALMS 19:1-4

Activity: Reflect on Psalms 19:1-4 and discuss how creativity expresses God's beauty and wonder.

What You Need:

• A Bible or Bible verse printout.
• A comfortable reading and discussion space.

Benefits/Skills Developed:

1. Spiritual Growth: Connecting creativity with spirituality deepens understanding.
2. Appreciation for Beauty: Encourages a sense of wonder and appreciation for the beauty in the world.

"IN THE STROKES OF OUR CREATIVITY, WE ECHO THE DIVINE ARTIST WHO SHAPED THE UNIVERSE."

ARTS AND CREATIVITY
WEEK 4

DAY 25: PAINT A SUNSET

Activity: Paint a serene sunset, exploring the warm and soothing colors of twilight.

What You Need:

- Acrylic or watercolor paints.
- Canvas or paper.
- Appreciation for changing skies.

Benefits/Skills Developed:

1. Artistic Expression: Painting allows for emotional expression.
2. Observational Skills: Observing sunsets enhances attention to detail.

"SUNSETS ARE GOD'S WAY OF PAINTING THE SKY WITH HIS LOVE, A BREATHTAKING MASTERPIECE TO REMIND US OF HIS PRESENCE."

ARTS AND CREATIVITY
WEEK 4

DAY 26: PLAYDOUGH CREATIONS

Activity: Sculpt a beautiful tree, farm, or rainbow with clay or playdough, let your imagination run free with vibrant colors and unique designs.

What You Need:

• Clay or playdough in various vibrant colors.
• Work surface or mat.
• Imagination!

Benefits/Skills Developed:

1. Creativity: Sparks creativity and artistic expression as you craft your own stunning natural scenes or colorful rainbows.

2. Fine Motor Skills: Enhances fine motor skills through the molding and shaping of clay or playdough into intricate details.

3. Imagination: Encourages imaginative thinking, allowing you to create whimsical and imaginative landscapes that reflect your inner creativity.

"FAMILY IS THE GALLERY WHERE LOVE AND CREATIVITY ARE PROUDLY DISPLAYED."

ART AND CREATIVITY
WEEK 4

DAY 27/28: RESET & REST

Art and Creativity - Sabbath Rest Suggestions

1. **Creative Sabbath Crafts:** Dedicate your Sabbath afternoon to creating art and crafts as a family.

2. **Family Art Show:** Showcase your creative works during a family art show, discussing what each piece represents.

3. **Bible Story Time:** Explore Psalms 19:1-4 and discuss how creativity is an expression of God's beauty.

4. **Challah Flavor:** Prepare a carob and coconut confetti challah for a sweet and creative twist on your Sabbath table.

"ON THE SABBATH, MOTHERS FILL THEIR CUPS WITH GOD'S LOVE AND FIND RENEWED STRENGTH TO CONTINUE THEIR LOVING JOURNEY."

"THROUGH THE SABBATH'S EMBRACE, MOTHERS FIND REST, RENEWAL, AND THE UNWAVERING STRENGTH TO CONQUER LIFE'S CHALLENGES WITH RESILIENCE AND GRACE."

PREP FOR ANOTHER MONTH
WEEK 4

DAY 29: RESET ROOMS & SHELVES

Activity: Declutter and reorganize your creative spaces, ensuring everything is ready for future fun.

What You Need:

• Cleaning supplies and organization tools.
• Teamwork and a fresh start.

Benefits/Skills Developed:

1. Organization: Teaches the importance of tidiness and order.
2. Teamwork: Promotes collaboration and shared responsibility.

"TIDYING UP IS MORE THAN JUST CLEANING; IT'S A RITUAL OF CLEARING THE CLUTTER, MAKING SPACE FOR NEW BEGINNINGS, AND FINDING PEACE IN SIMPLICITY."

PREP FOR NEXT MONTH
WEEK 4

DAY 30: DOWNLOAD MONTH 2

Activity: Prepare for more exciting worldschooling adventures by downloading the next month's activities.

What You Need:

• Access to the next month's worldschooling activities.
• Excitement for upcoming adventures!

Get ready for another month of fantastic worldschooling adventures with your family! Download the next set of activities and let the learning and creativity continue.

"PREPARING FOR ANOTHER MONTH IS LIKE TURNING THE PAGE IN THE BOOK OF LIFE, WITH BLANK DAYS AWAITING OUR STORIES AND ADVENTURES."

Autumn Season

**MONTH 2
GRATITUDE &
KINDNESS**

- Introduction to basic concepts like "thank you" and "please"
- Nature walks to explore and marvel at God's creation
- Simple prayers before meals and bedtime
- Reading picture books with themes of gratitude and wonder
-Tiny hands big acts of kindness
-Global Gratitude
-Counting our Blessings

ONE LAST THING

As you near the end of this beautiful 30-day adventure with your little one, I want to remind you of something truly important – you are free to go at your own pace and adapt these activities to fit the rhythm of your home and life. The journey of nurturing your toddler's curiosity and growing together in faith is a personal one, and it should always feel right for you and your precious child.

I created this guide with a deep passion and purpose. It came from a place of wanting to share the possibilities of solo parenting in the context of homeschooling. I often felt like the resources available online were geared towards two-parent households, and I wanted to show that it's not only possible but also incredibly rewarding to embark on this journey as a full-time solo parent. I have been inspired by my own experiences, challenges, and triumphs, and I hope to inspire you in turn.

My true prayer is that this guide finds its way into the hands of those who need it most – the defeated and struggling single, and stay-at-home mothers who may not have the family they imagined but possess the strength to make the family they have a thriving and loving one. You are blessed, and your journey is an inspiration to us all.

ONE LAST THING
...Continued

And as you embrace this path, I hope the traditions I shared, such as baking homemade bread and observing the Sabbath, can find a special place in your home. There is truly nothing sweeter than the smell of homemade bread wafting through your home, filling it with warmth and comfort. And the sound of praise, whether it be through songs, prayers, or simply expressing gratitude, can transform your home into a Heavenly Home of love and faith. May these traditions become the heartbeats of your household, reminding you of the beauty and simplicity of the moments you've shared.

So, dear parent, whether you choose to revisit these activities in any order that suits your household or sprinkle them throughout your days, know that the bond you are nurturing and the faith you are instilling are invaluable gifts that will last a lifetime. Embrace this journey with an open heart, cherish every moment, and remember that you are never alone on this path in Gods Classroom.

With heartfelt blessings,

Sabrina

FOCUCCIA RECIPE

Ingredients:

- 420 ml warm water
- 1 teaspoon (4g) instant yeast
- 2 teaspoons (10g) sea salt
- 1 teaspoon (5g) honey
- 1 tablespoon extra virgin olive oil
- 500 g spelt flour

Preparation:

1. In a bowl, mix warm water, instant yeast, sea salt, honey, and olive oil until well combined.
2. Add spelt flour to the wet ingredients, stirring until a sticky dough forms. Cover the bowl and let it rest for 10 minutes.
3. With very wet hands, fold the dough from north to south, turning the bowl clockwise. Repeat this process four times. Let the dough rest for 5 minutes then repeat process another 3 times resting for 5 mins in between each set.
4. After the last folding, coat the dough with a layer of olive oil. Cover with a shower cap or plastic wrap.
5. Allow the dough to rise for 1.5-2 hours or until it has doubled in size.
6. Optionally, place the dough in the fridge overnight for added flavor.
7. Preheat your oven to 220°C (425°F).
8. Gently transfer it to a parchment-lined baking sheet.
9. Using the 4x folding method, fold the dough over itself from all four sides, creating layers.
10. Allow the folded dough to rest for about 15-20 minutes.
11. Bake in the preheated oven for 20-25 minutes or until the focaccia is golden brown and sounds hollow when tapped.
12. Remove from the oven and let it cool slightly before slicing.

Enjoy your spelt flour focaccia with the unique texture achieved through the folding method and the overnight refrigeration!

CHALLAH RECIPE

Ingredients:

- 1.25 oz yeast (7 g)
- ½ cup granulated sugar (110 g), plus an extra pinch for the yeast
- 1 cup warm water (245 mL), and 3 tablespoons more for the dough
- 6 tablespoons melted coconut oil, plus more for greasing
- 2 teaspoons baking powder
- 3 cups all-purpose flour (375 g), plus extra as needed
- 1 ½ teaspoons salt

Preparation:

1. In a medium bowl, mix yeast with a pinch of sugar. Pour 1 cup warm water over it, allowing the bowl to stir itself. Rest for 5 minutes until the yeast is bubbly, then add 2 tablespoons of melted coconut oil.
2. In another bowl, combine 3 tablespoons melted coconut oil, 3 tablespoons warm water, and baking powder.
3. In a large bowl, whisk 3 cups of flour, salt, and the remaining ½ cup of sugar. Stir in the coconut oil and yeast mixtures. Gradually add up to 1 cup of flour, kneading until smooth (you might not need all the flour).
4. Knead until the dough isn't sticking to the bowl. Transfer to a large bowl greased with coconut oil, cover with a damp towel, and let it rise on the counter for 2 hours or until doubled.
5. Punch down the dough, knead gently, and shape into a log. Cut into pieces based on your braiding plan.
6. Braid the dough, transfer to a baking sheet, cover with a damp towel, and let rise for 1 hour.
7. Preheat the oven to 325°F (165°C).
8. Lightly brush the challah with melted coconut oil, bake for 25-30 minutes, brushing with more coconut oil halfway through, until golden brown. Check for doneness by tapping the bottom; if it sounds hollow, it's done!
9. Cool completely on a wire rack before slicing. Enjoy your coconut oil-infused challah!

STRENGTH AND HONOR
ARE HER CLOTHING; SHE
SHALL REJOICE IN TIME TO
COME.
SHE OPENS HER MOUTH
WITH WISDOM, AND ON
HER TONGUE IS THE LAW
OF KINDNESS.
SHE WATCHES OVER THE
WAYS OF HER
HOUSEHOLD, AND DOES
NOT EAT THE BREAD OF
IDLENESS.
HER CHILDREN RISE UP AND
CALL HER BLESSED;-
PROVERBS 31:25 (NKJV)

RESOURCES

BOOKS

PODCASTS

THE HOLY BIBLE (KJV)
COLLINS (2011)

email- hhwschool@gmail.com
for our recommendations

WOMAN'S STUDY BIBLE (NIV)
TN BIBLES (2017)

CHILD GUIDANCE
ELLEN G. WHITE ESTATE (2010)

INSTAGRAM INSPIRATION

email - hhworldschool@gmail.com
for our recommendations

THE MONTESSORI METHOD
SERENA DE MITCHELI (2023)

CHILD EDUCATION
CHARLOTTE M. MANSON
LIVING BOOK PRESS (2017)

RAISING FREE PEOPLE
AKILAH S. RICHARDS
PM PRESS (2020)

Disclaimer:

The mention of podcasts, and Instagram handles in this ebook are for reference purposes only. We are not affiliated with, endorsed by, or endorsing the mentioned Instagram accounts. Any opinions or views expressed are solely those of the author and do not reflect the views of the Instagram account owners. We do not claim any ownership or association with these accounts.

THE BRAVE LEARNER
JULIE BOGART
PENGUIN PUBLISHING GROUP (2019)

HOMESCHOOL BRAVELY
JAMIE ERICKSON
MOODY PRESS (2019)

MEMORY MAKING MUM
JESSICA SMARTT
THOMAS NELSON PUBLISHERS (2019)

REFERENCES

Page 8: Philippians 4:13 (NKJV) - Thomas Nelson, 2012

Page 8: Proverbs 9:10 (NKJV) - Thomas Nelson, 2018

Page 12: Proverbs 2:6 (NKJV) - Thomas Nelson, 2018

Page 18: ""Child Guidance by Ellen G. White - The Stanborough Press Ltd, 2012

Page 14: "School Education" by Charlotte Mason - Living Book Press, 2017

Page 18: Proverbs 22:6 (NKJV) - Thomas Nelson, 2018

Page 21: "The Secret of Childhood" by Maria Montessori - Random House Inc; New edition, 1982

Page 23: Philippians 4:13 (NKJV) - Thomas Nelson, 2018

Page 41: Leviticus 23:3 (NKJV) - Thomas Nelson, 2018

Page 48: Matthew 11:28 (NKJV) - Thomas Nelson, 2018

Page 68:Foccucia Recipe - Instagram @ _lacebakes_

Page 69: Challah Recipe -Challah Hub @ Tasty.co

Page 70: Proverbs 31:25 (NKJV) - Thomas Nelson, 2018

Page 79: Mark 16:1 (NKJV) - Thomas Nelson, 2018

GLOSSARY

Traditional/Classical Education: Emphasizes grammar, logic, and rhetoric systematically, often focusing on classical literature and subjects like Latin.

Montessori Method: Developed by Maria Montessori, it encourages child-led learning in a prepared environment with a focus on hands-on activities and self-directed exploration.

Unschooling: A child-driven approach where learning is based on the child's interests, without a fixed curriculum or schedule.

Charlotte Mason Method: Emphasizes living books, nature study, and short lessons to provide a broad and generous education.

Waldorf/Steiner Education: Developed by Rudolf Steiner, it emphasizes creativity, imagination, and a holistic approach to education, often integrating arts and crafts.

Unit Studies: Focuses on a specific topic, integrating various subjects around that central theme for in-depth exploration.

Eclectic Homeschooling: Combines elements from various methods, allowing parents to tailor their approach based on the child's needs and learning style.

Online or Virtual Schooling: Utilizes online resources and virtual classrooms, often following a structured curricul um provided by an online school.

Religious or Faith-Based Education: Integrates religious teachings and values into the educational curriculum.

Classical Conversations: A classical education approach with a focus on community-based learning, often involving group discussions and activities.

Reggio Emilia Approach: Originating in Italy, it emphasizes a child's natural curiosity and involves collaboration between students, teachers, and parents.

High Scope Method: A child-centered approach that emphasizes active participation, hands-on experiences, and the importance of daily routines.

Eclectic/Relaxed Homeschooling: A flexible approach where parents pick and choose from various methods and resources based on their child's needs and interests.

Travel-Based Learning: Utilizes travel experiences as the primary means of education, exposing children to different cultures, languages, and historical sites.

Project World Schooling: Learning through immersive projects, often integrating subjects into real-world scenarios and hands-on experiences.

Cultural Exchange Programs: Involves participating in cultural exchange programs, allowing children to learn from different societies and communities.

Multiple Intelligences Theory: Tailors education to different types of intelligences identified by Howard Gardner, such as linguistic, logical-mathematical, spatial, musical, etc.

Thomas Jefferson Education: Emphasizes leadership education, focusing on classics, character development, and mentoring.

Language Immersion: Learning through immersion in different language environments, often through travel or connecting with native speakers.

Global Online Learning: Utilizing online resources and courses that provide a global perspective, connecting with students from around the world.

Hybrid Homeschooling: Blends traditional classroom learning with homeschooling. Students attend classes part-time at a physical school and homeschool for the remaining time.

Socratic Method: Based on the teaching philosophy of Socrates, it emphasizes dialogue and discussion to stimulate critical thinking and deeper understanding of concepts.

Botany: The branch of biology that focuses on the study of plants.

Geology: The science that explores the Earth's structure, composition, and processes that shape its surface.

Biology: The scientific study of living organisms and their interactions.

Future 30 Day Plans

Calling all adventurous mums of toddlers! Sign up today and give your little ones the world as their classroom. Don't miss out on this enriching journey of discovery!

Autumn Season

MONTH 1
CREATION
WONDERS

MONTH 2
HARVESTING
JOY

MONTH 3
GRATITUDE &
KINDNESS

Winter Season

MONTH 4
JOURNEY TO
THE
MANGER

MONTH 5
STORIES OF
FAITH

MONTH 6
LOVE IN
COLOUR

Spring Season

MONTH 7
NATURE'S
SYMPHONY

MONTH 8
COUNTING
CREATURES

MONTH 9
GOD'S
GARDEN

Summer Season

MONTH 10
SKY &
SEA

MONTH 11
NATURES
TREASURE

MONTH 12
GLOBAL
ARTS

eBook Introductary Month 1
SIGN UP TODAY!

email: hhworldschool@gmail.com

Subscription Plans Available

30 Day Meal Plan

Calling all plant-based mums of toddlers! Embark on a nourishing journey with us. Download our 30-day stress-free meal plan that perfectly aligns with our Month 1 theme. Give your little ones a healthy and delicious start!

Coming Soon to our Etsy Store

email hhworldschool@gmail.com

Promo Code: EBOOKFAN for buyers discount

30 Day Devontional

Calling all nurturing faith-based Mamas! Dive into a deeper connection with your spirituality. Download our enlightening 30-day devotional, thoughtfully tailored to align with our monthly themes and daily activities. Strengthen your bond while deepening your faith journey together.

Coming Soon to our Etsy Store

email: hhworldschool@gmail.com

Promo Code: EBOOKFAN for buyers discount

30 Day Journal

Calling all nurturing faith-based Mamas! Dive into a deeper connection with your spirituality. Download our enlightening 30-day devotional, thoughtfully tailored to align with our monthly themes and daily activities. Strengthen your bond while deepening your faith journey together.

Coming Soon to our Etsy Store

email: hhworldschool@gmail.com

Promo Code: EBOOKFAN for buyers discount

AROUND THE WORLD FOR
CHRISTMAS

SONGS, STORIES & TRADITIONS
FROM 12 COUNTRIES

Heavenly Home Worldschool

Download yours Free at
www.heavenlyhomeworldschool.com

Harmonize Your Holiday: 12
Hymns of Tradition, Peace,
Hope, and Celebration

Happy worldschooling

🖤Heavenly Home Worldschool

"GO INTO ALL THE WORLD
AND PREACH THE GOSPEL TO
ALL CREATION." – MARK 16:1
(NKJV)

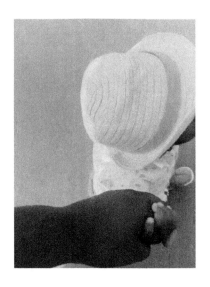

Faith
Learn
Explore

Printed in Great Britain
by Amazon

30505931R00044